Bruce—A Yorkie's Tale

Bruce—A Yorkie's Tale

CJ Hackett

VANTAGE PRESS
New York

FIRST EDITION

Published by Vantage Press, Inc.
419 Park Ave. South, New York, NY 10016

Manufactured in the United States of America
ISBN: 0-533-15082-5

Library of Congress Catalog Card No.: 2004098324

0 9 8 7 6 5 4 3 2 1

Bruce—A Yorkie's Tale

My name is Bruce, and I am a Yorkshire Terrier, or a "Yorkie", for short. I was born in Puppy City, in Brooklyn, New York, on July 20, 1992, and was adopted by a nice Greek family, who named me Bruce, on October 3 of that same year. Actually, it was the girl in the family who christened me with that name, all because she was a huge fan of Bruce Springsteen. As time went on, everyone in the family started calling me some strange variations of "Bruce", such as "Budgie", and even now as "Boopie". I was never too crazy about "Budgie", because that sounded like the name of a roly-poly fat kid from the *Little Rascals*. And "Boopie" sounds too girlish for me, a proud male dog. But, just to keep my masters amused, I have had to answer to "Budgie", then later to "Boopie", and when my masters are angry or stern with me, to "Bruce".

For those of you who are not familiar with us proud "Yorkies", we are petite, but strong and fierce watchdogs and hunters. I will protect my master(s) with all my might, just as long as he or she provides me with enough food and shelter. It's sort of like a "you scratch my back, I'll scratch yours" type of arrangement.

When I was first adopted by my big, fat Greek family, I was small and quite scared. I wasn't potty-trained properly and had trouble going to the bathroom. I also could not sleep well at night because I was hearing strange noises in the house. They kept me in a small area in the hallway that was divided by two big boards. I guess the family did not want me to see where they stashed their goodies. I used to "yap" a lot, saying that I wanted to get away from the boarded area because I was feeling claus- trophobic. The girl in the family used to come into that area, pick me up, bring me to her bedroom and lull me to sleep. Let me tell you, that felt good.

It took me a while, a few weeks at the most, but I was finally being potty-trained and was going to the bathroom regularly. The girl in the family was the first to see me lift up my leg to go to the bathroom. Once she saw that, she told everyone else and everyone applauded my natural behavior. How embarrassing is that! But now, all I had to do was say, "Yap-yap," and someone in the family would let me go outdoors and then I did my business. Everyone in the household was quite pleased about this.

After I was properly potty-trained and felt better, the family brought me to the veterinarian to be neutered. Imagine that, my newly adoptive family betrayed me by getting me fixed. The procedure itself was not too bad; but I was in pain for days afterwards, and my feelings were extremely hurt. I was actually plotting on getting back at my new family. I haven't done anything drastic yet, but I have caused them some embarrassment from time to time, but more on that later.

While I was recovering from the procedure, the girl in my new family, her name is Cornelia, took it upon herself to cuddle and comfort me. I must admit I was completely surprised by her generosity, and the warmth she provided me with after being so close to her made me realize, beyond all of Dog-Heaven, that this was the one person I must protect at all times.

My Greek family lived on Foster Avenue in Brooklyn; not the greatest of neighborhoods, but it was livable. I was living with Cornelia, her parents, Ted and Ourania, her twin brother, Nick, and an older brother. Nick lived upstairs. Constantine, the older brother, lived downstairs in the finished basement, and Cornelia and her parents lived on the main floor. Me being a naive and inexperienced pup in those days (not that I have changed much now), I used to bark at anything that would walk the streets, including UPS carriers and mailmen. For some strange reason, I had a tendency to believe that mail carriers were "bearers of bad news" (usually they have our bills that have to be paid) and that I should protect my masters (whoever they may be) and prevent the mailperson from coming near the house.

There were times, however, when everyone in the family would be away from the house at the same time, leaving me behind to watch over the place. Constantine and Nick would visit one of their friends, and Cornelia and her parents would go to the movies or out to dinner. All of the entrances to the house would be locked, of course, but I would stay at home anyway to guard the place. Little did I know that restaurants and moviehouses did not allow dogs or any other pets, for that matter, in their establishments. Now, that's discrimination. But that was all right, my masters used to leave me with plenty of water and dog food (ugh!) when they went out.

So I would just roam around the house, making sure everything was A-O.K., and then I would smell something very peculiar coming from the dining room table. My masters would leave their chairs by the table, so I was able to jump up onto a chair and then onto the table. And there I would see something that was about a foot long and smelled delicious. I had seen my masters eat these things before; they were called bananas. My masters would peel the skin off and eat the inside of it. Everyone in the house ate them, so they must be good! So I decided to try one.

Let me tell you, it was extremely difficult to unwrap these things when all you have are your four paws and your teeth, but they sure were good! So good, I had more than I could handle. I was starting to feel sick, and when I saw the mess I had made trying to peel these suckas, I felt even sicker. I tried to hide the evidence, but I felt cramps in my tummy. I went into Cornelia's bedroom to lay down for a few minutes, just to recover for a bit, then go back and clean up the place. I felt so nauseous that I went to sleep.

When I woke up, Constantine and Nick were standing over me, horrified that I left behind such a mess. I was like, "Go away, let me sleep." Then, Cornelia and her parents came home, and her brothers told them what happened. They were all yelling at me, and laughing at me. I was like, "Where's the Pepto-Bismol for dogs?" I was so sick, I had the cramps in my tummy for a whole week. Why didn't anyone tell me that dogs were not allowed to eat bananas? I don't blame myself for this, I blame my masters. They should not have left those things where I could get at them. So there!

The mother in the family, Ourania, used to leave her pocketbook on the floor. I would notice the pocketbook sitting there and I would walk over to it and check it out. I would pretend to be a detective and sniff out and search for anything that looked suspicious. After all, that was my job, right? But I would almost always smell something that had a pleasant scent inside the pocketbook and would see if I could locate where this smell was coming from. So, while no one was looking, I started to sniff the outside of the pocketbook, then laid it flat on the floor and started to inch my way toward the middle of the bag using my front paws and my nose.

My nose can sniff out trouble, but it can also get me into trouble. Anyhow, after much digging, I finally found the source of that pleasant odor: a small pack of Wrigley's chewing gum. I was like, "Wow. This stuff smells so good, so it also has to taste good, too." So I pulled the pack of gum out of the pocketbook, somehow pull a slice of gum out of the pack, and noticed there was paper wrapped around the gum. I'm thinking, *What the hell is this?* So, I proceeded to use my front paws and teeth to unwrap the gum. Finally, when I got the wrapper off, I started to chew on the gum. I was like, "This is good, but how come it doesn't dissolve in my mouth like any other food I eat? This thing is so chewy, I might have to swallow it whole and hide the evidence so no one would notice."

Just as soon as I thought of that, some of the gum got caught on the hair below my mouth. "Uh-oh," I said to myself. No sooner did I think that, than Ourania came along, stood over me and asked what I was doing. I looked up at her rather innocently, but I could see that she knew what I had done. So she knelt down, saw that I had gum all around the hair of my mouth, laughed, and said, "Caught ya!" Then, she and Constantine had to cut the hair around my mouth to get rid of the gum. Like I said before, my nose, or rather, my nosiness, can seek out trouble, but it can also get me into trouble, as well.

My masters prided themselves upon the fact that they always tried to keep their home as clean and neat as possible. This was not to say that some of my masters' neighbors cared enough to be as neat as they. In fact, their next-door neighbor, who was a deaf-mute, was also such a slob he made Oscar Madison look neater than Felix Unger. He was so messy that his house actually had mice in it! And somehow, those mice used to come into our house.

The first time I ever saw a mouse, I thought he was soooo cute, I wanted to adopt him! Hey, if my adopted parents can have a pet, which was me, why can't I adopt a pet mouse? But when I saw how unruly and disloyal this mouse was to me, I decided not to get involved with them.

Why, Cornelia and her parents had mousetraps around their house just in case one of them came in for a visit. Very often, though, a mouse did get himself caught in a trap. And let me tell you, it was not a pretty sight! Then either Cornelia or one of her parents had the dubious honor of burying that poor dead mouse in a garbage can in the street. I thought, *What a horrible way to go.* Then I thought, *These mice are small and furry, just like me. Does this mean that I, too, will be unceremoniously tossed into the garbage when my time comes?* I shudder at the thought that my human masters, who bury their loved ones with honor and dignity, would stoop so low as to get rid of their faithful pet in the manner of an old shoe, to be forgotten by all. I sincerely hope it will not come down to that. I must resolve to myself to be as loyal and faithful as I can possibly be to my masters, so that I, too, will be buried with honor and dignity, and be remembered by all when that Big Dog in the sky comes calling for me.

Nick had purchased a house in Florida, and Cornelia and her parents had to fly down in an airplane to get there, and they used to take me with them. Now, let it be known that I have a certain fear of heights, and that my being on an airplane meant only one of two things; either the pilots sedate me, or there would be a real-life Airport movie disaster. The airlines decided to sedate me, and off we would all go to Florida.

Florida was nice, not my cup of Mighty Dog puppy-chow; but I did have my share of fun there. Nick's house was situated in a cul-de-sac, with plenty of property to roam around in and get this; no fences! Being a puppy, I had this incredible urge to "explore strange new yards, to seek out new life and new strangers, to boldly go where no dog had gone before." And boy, did I take advantage of that! Whenever I had to go to the bathroom, I went outside, did what I had to do, and then, it was play-time! Hide-and-go-seek was a very popular game with me. I used to have my masters and their neighbors chase after me. It was fun watching them huffing and puffing trying to catch me. Finally, after about twenty minutes of watching them sweat and curse me out, I would give in to them. Otherwise, I wouldn't have any dinner that night.

Nick also had a sunken pool that was screened in to keep the bugs out. I would sit in the pool area from time-to-time and watch my masters jump in the pool and have fun getting themselves wet. I could not understand how they could enjoy the pool but would hate getting wet when it rained. Hell, I didn't even like it when it rained. So one time, when no one was looking, I sort of "fell" into the pool. Let me tell you, that water was deep and COLD. I was like, "I'm in the pool now, so what do I do? How do I get out?" I started to swim, or doggie-paddle, around the pool looking for a way out. I was getting nervous because there was no way out! Eventually my masters, who were obviously looking for me, saw me in the pool, and screamed. I was thinking, *What are you guys screaming about? Someone get me out of this water because my arms are getting tired.* Finally, Constantine jumped into the pool and hauled me out. When I came out, I was soaking wet. My masters yelled at me one minute, and laughed at me the next. They actually thought my ordeal was cute. I was embarrassed. From that moment on, I hated getting wet, whether it was from being in a pool, or being outdoors in the rain, or taking a bath.

Speaking of baths; I know for a fact that a lot of us dogs do not like taking them. The reasons are varied and sometimes personal, but I don't like taking them because I don't like getting wet, and I can't stand the smell of the soap. I mean, what male dog in his right mind likes to walk around smelling of perfume? Whenever Constantine, Cornelia and their mother were getting ready to give me a bath in their tub, I give them hell. From the time they pick me up, put me in the tub, soak me with the water, lather me with the soap, then soap me again, I'm fighting them tooth and nail (I don't always win, of course) and I splash the water right back at them. And you know what they do? They laugh, and say I look so cute and smell nice! I'm supposed to be a watchdog! Who said watchdogs are supposed to smell nice? Anyway, that lasted for a short time, because when they saw that my hair was getting long, and they didn't want to cut my hair because they thought they might cut me by accident, they started to take me to a dog-grooming salon. Can you imagine? A dog-grooming salon! Every time I go to one of those places, I feel so embarrassed, I want to disown my masters!

Nick's house also had a lot of rooms, so one day I decided to check them out. There was a lot of closet space in that house, and me being a nosy little puppy, I decided to see what was in the closets. In the closet of one of the guest rooms, I found a pair of white sandals. So, being in the playful mood that I was in, I grabbed one sandal and went under the bed with it. I then decided to play with it and ended up chewing off the strap of the sandal. When I realized what I had done, I was hoping and praying that no one was really going to miss these sandals. Turns out, I was wrong. They belonged to Cornelia, and when she saw what I did, she screamed at the top of her lungs at me. She was so mad, she didn't talk to me for two whole days. I even had to sleep on the floor in the guest bedroom because she wouldn't let me on the bed. After that, Cornelia felt sorry for me. I tried to make it up to her but, being a dog, and not getting an allowance, I couldn't give her any money for the sandals. It took a while, but eventually she forgave me for destroying her favorite shoes.

Nick also had a bay window in his living room that was draped by vertical blinds on the inside of the house. The blinds were so high they practically covered the walls from top to bottom. You could still see out that window, of course, all you had to do was slide the blinds over. But one day, while Constantine was in Florida, he and Nick had gone out, leaving me all alone in his house. I heard a noise coming from outside the bay window, and wanted to see what it was.

I ran to the window and started barking. I didn't hear anything after that, but I was still curious, so I tried to look through the vertical blinds by trying to squeeze through them. Somehow, my front paw got stuck on a chain on the bottom of the blinds. I tried to pull my paw away from the chain. But every time I tried to walk back from the blinds, the chain kept getting tighter around my paw. And it hurt! I was like, "Uh-oh! What did I do now?"

Luckily, Nick and Constantine returned home a few minutes later. They said they noticed the blinds in the bay window moving, and didn't know what was going on until they came home and saw me, trapped like a rat, with my front paw stuck on the chain. Nick and Constantine had a hard time freeing me, so they had to cut a piece of the chain to let me go. After that, they thought it would be wise not to leave me alone in the house because they felt I was too "immature and dopey" and would get into too much trouble by myself. Hey! I heard a noise, alright? I went to investigate. That's what we dogs do, O.K.? I can't help if that evil chain was trying to get me into trouble, and making it look like I'm the bad guy here.

One thing my masters really enjoyed doing was getting together for an outdoor barbecue. Here, they would have hamburgers and hot dogs and sausage, and cook them on an open barbecue grill out in the backyard. Everybody's pitching in, molding the hamburgers from Ground Round meat, and putting them on a tray to be put on the grill, as well as putting the hot dogs and sausage on separate trays. This looks like fun, and everyone always seems to have a good time sitting around, eating and talking. But since no one wants to talk with me, and I always seem to get the last bite out of a hamburger and/or a hot dog, I decided to help myself to the first bite.

11

Constantine had made hamburgers out of the Ground Round and put them on a tray. Then he put the tray on a table near the grill and walked away. I sat there, looked around and saw that no one was looking, jumped on the chair that was next to the table, and helped myself to the raw hamburger meat. I mean, I was so hungry, I ate the whole thing.

Cornelia and Constantine came back out from being inside the house carrying the hot dogs and sausage, and placed those two items on the table, when one of them realized the hamburger meat was missing. One asked the other if either one had left the meat inside the house. Then Constantine noticed bits of the meat on the table, and the both of them looked at me. If I didn't have such a bad tummy-ache from eating that meat so fast, I would have given Cornelia and Constantine my best innocent puppy-dog look ever. But they saw right through me, and yelled at me, and called me a bad dog.

I meekly walked around the corner and plopped myself down, too sick to walk another foot. I tried to close my eyes and go to sleep, but within minutes everyone had found out what I had done and started scolding me. I was like, "People, simmer down, will ya? I'm feeling sick now, and I want to sleep it off." A few hours later, of course, everyone had forgiven me, but my latest bad deed had stayed in their memory banks forever. Now, when people want a good laugh about me, they almost always bring up the hamburger story.

As I had mentioned before, Florida was nice, but

nothing beats living in good old New York City; or in Brooklyn, where my masters grew up. The house on Foster Avenue was big, had enough room for all of us and the neighborhood, being mixed ethnically, was really not too bad. Constantine, who lived downstairs, had a girlfriend, as did Nick, who lived upstairs. Me, I was content being with Cornelia and her parents. In fact, I actually felt safe living there with all these people. I could actually live there forever.

One hot August night in 1993, Cornelia had a date. No one was more surprised about this than me. Cornelia hardly goes out on dates, but this one night she had a date with this dude who lived with his parents on Staten Island. Cornelia seemed to have had a good time, and I was amazed that she invited her date to meet with her parents. I started thinking, *Let me check this dude out, and see what he's made of.*

He came to the house one night, saw me for the first time, and said to Cornelia, "Oh, I didn't know you had a dog." I was very insulted when I heard that. I was saying to myself, "Look here, Bozo! I am not just a dog! I am the family security personnel as well as their faithful companion. Don't you ever forget that!" I started to bark, just to see what he was going to do, and was told to be quiet. Cornelia's date, whose name is John, said that I was cute. I looked at John, who wore glasses, and thought, "Jeez, I hope Mr. Four-Eyes here doesn't get fresh with my master." Against my wishes, Cornelia went out that night with John, and I was beginning to wonder if this was the start of something new.

My early fears were realized when Cornelia began to go out more and more with John. On top of that, Nick was getting serious with his girlfriend, as was Constantine with his. It was becoming more apparent to me that I was no longer the center of attention.

I started thinking, "What the hell did I do to cause this?" Oh sure, every once in a while someone would say how cute I looked, but deep down, I was really feeling neglected. Hey, dogs have feelings too, you know! We dogs go through the same emotional traumas as you humans do. We feel pain, emotionally and physically, and we are happy when things go our way. One common misconception humans have about dogs is that we canines do not have the capacity to think enough. Well, let me tell you, we dogs do think A LOT, and not just about where our next meal is going to come from, either. I am constantly thinking of ways to protect the family. I think about crime in New York City, its economy, and global affairs. Once in a while, I would even think about Einstein's Theory of Relativity (got ya!). Well, maybe I understand a little bit about that theory. But I am constantly thinking about Newton's Law of Gravity (gotcha again!).

Another misconception humans have of dogs is that we canines cannot communicate with humans, that we dogs "bark" instead of talking. Hey, did it ever occur to you humans that when we dogs bark, we ARE talking? We dogs know what we are saying, it's you humans that do not understand OUR language. And not all barks are the same. One bark means one thing, three barks in a row mean something else, while seven barks in succession means, "Look out, here comes the mailman!"

Then there are the different dialects of a bark. One loud bark means, "Hey, I'm here, so pay attention to me!" Whereas one little yap means, "Yoo-hoo! Here I am!" Still another misconception humans have is they always believe that whatever they say to us, we don't understand them. Not true. We dogs understand everything you humans are saying, in any language. We understand all of your conversations and arguments. We understand your fears and concerns. When you listen to the news, we listen to the news (by the way, your taxes are too high!). It is just that when you humans talk to us, and order us to do things, we dogs have to determine if your orders are in our best interests first, then we decide whether or not to carry them out. Sometimes, I just like to sit there, and listen to you practically beg me to do things I don't normally want to do. You humans look so cute begging.

Being a young pup, I often wondered what I would be doing if Nick, Constantine and Cornelia finally left their parents' home. Would I go with one of them, or stay behind and be the parents' guardian? At the time, no one had mentioned anything about getting married and moving on. It seemed Monday through Friday, the household was rather quiet because some people had to go to work and/or school; but Saturday and Sunday, forget it. Everyone would be in and out of the house for hours at a time. I would count on the toenails of my paws how many times Cornelia and John would go out together on the weekends.

Also, being the only dog in the entire household meant that each night was a different night to be with any one of the three couples, or with Cornelia. But for the most part, I was with the parents because they were older and were more in need of my security services. Their house was my domain to guard, and I don't care who you are, no one enters the house or stays there without my checking you out first.

One February night in 1994, and I do believe it was a Monday night, on Valentine's Day, John came to the house to take Cornelia out for dinner. The fact that it was a Monday night made everything seem suspicious. Hardly anyone goes out for dinner on a Monday night. But John showed up at the house looking rather handsome in a suit and Cornelia greeted him wearing a very nice dress. Now let it be known that we dogs do not celebrate Valentine's Day, but we know that you humans do it your own very special and crazy way, but to go out for dinner on a Monday night? There was something strange going on, and I am not talking about the smelly cat next door, either.

So Cornelia and John went out that night. They came back almost three hours later, with Cornelia having a big smile on her face. It was the moment I've been dreading all along; Cornelia and John announced their intention to be married! But first John had to ask Cornelia's dad, Ted, for her hand in marriage. When he said yes I felt so sick to my stomach, you have no idea. How could my nice Greek family betray me by letting Cornelia get away? Everyone else was so happy about the announcement, they were all hugging and kissing each other, and there I was, feeling so badly betrayed and hurt. Now I know how Julius Caesar must have felt!

And then, on top of whatever other extraordinary thing that went on that night, Cornelia and John went back out together again, this time I guess to go to Staten Island, to inform his parents of the unexpected announcement. They came back two hours later, leaving John's parents also surprised and happy about the announcement. Everyone was happy to hear the news. Everyone, that is, except me.

You're probably thinking how selfish I am not to be happy for Cornelia. Nothing could be further from the truth. I was extremely happy for her. It was just that when the day comes that she goes off and lives with John, the once-united household will no longer be united. On top of that, Nicky and his girlfriend decided that they, too, were going to be married. I was like, "Uh-oh, is Constantine next?"

The days after the twins' wedding announcements were more serious than usual. Everyone in the family began to call everyone else in the family to inform them of the twins' plans. Nick and his fiancée, Dena, had arranged to be married before Cornelia and John, and then they were going to move to Florida. Cornelia and John set up their wedding date to be a full fourteen months after they became engaged. I was thinking, *Now I have plenty of time to stop this wedding from taking place and split-*

ting up the family. I was trying to come up with the right words, or barks, so I could communicate with Cornelia not to break up the family this way. But every time I said something, or barked, everyone thought I wanted a dog biscuit, or wanted to go out, or I was told to shut up. That's the trouble with you humans, you just don't listen very well!

One thing I am not going to reveal is what goes on in my master(s) bedrooms. After all, that is a bit of a private matter in any household, and that's how it will stay; private. But I will say one thing; I probably have seen more hanky-pankying at my young age than most of you humans do in forty years. I don't want to sound like I'm bragging or anything like that, even though I am. But after watching my master(s), it seemed like so much fun I often copy it by using just a blanket. That's right, just a blanket. Try it sometime.

Anyway, getting back to Cornelia and John. The first few months after their announcement were solely focused on their wedding day; where the church services were going to be, the reception, and where they were going on their honeymoon. And finally, where they were going to live when they came back (that is, if they were still married when they came back). And how much all this was going to cost them! Cornelia's dad, Ted, jokingly said to them, "Why not elope, instead?" Here I am trying to think of a way to stop this wedding from happening, and Cornelia's dad wants to get rid of his daughter! I'm like, "Ted, you're not helping!"

Well, it took Cornelia and John a few months to get everything organized for their wedding day. Now, it was just a matter of waiting for that day to come. As I have mentioned before, their engagement period was a full fourteen months before they were to be married. That, to me, was a long time to be engaged, but plenty of time for me to make John's life a living hell. Every time I knew he was coming to the house, I would sneak up behind him and try to scare him by barking. Or, he would come into the house, sit down on the couch, and I would jump up onto his lap, and lick his face with my smelly dog breath. Nothing I would do seemed to work. Maybe I should just get used to the idea that my happy family would eventually break up.

Nick and Dena were married in October of 1994, and soon after that, moved to Florida. Nick vowed he would never come back to New York again to live. It was sad to see them leave. But I knew we would see them again soon, during the holiday season. Cornelia and John were busy trying to save up money for their wedding. Meanwhile, Ted and Ourania were busy working on plans of their own; plans that really started to make my hair turn gray. They were selling their house!

Now I was really getting sick to my stomach! How could Ted do this to me? First, Nick and Cornelia leave the house by way of getting married, then their parents decided to sell the house! I'm like, "Stop the world, I'm getting dizzy!" Now, what's going to happen to me?

With Nick gone, things around the house were quieter, yet more busy. Cornelia and John finally found a nice apartment to live in on Staten Island; in a much nicer environment. In fact, they found this place just about a month before they were to be wed. All this place needed for now was a good paint job and a decent rug. So John was at the apartment constantly, repainting the place. Constantine, as a wedding present to his only sister, decided to buy and install a new rug in the apartment. Constantine's girlfriend, Amanda, had a brother that did that kind of work, so one day during the week, while John was a work, Constantine and Amanda's brother went into the apartment and changed the carpeting! I thought that was so nice!

Cornelia's big day finally came, on Friday, April 28, 1995. Everyone woke up early, eager to start the day. Everyone, that is, except me; for I knew that this was the beginning of the end for everyone in 417 Foster Avenue to be living under the same roof. Everything was quiet until the early afternoon when the make-up lady came to help set Cornelia's hair and apply the make-up. That took over an hour to do. Then John's sister-in-law and niece came to the house, as did a friend of Cornelia's. I gave everyone a complete and thorough inspection before I allowed them to see Cornelia, and still everyone said I was cute.

Then the wedding photographer came, and what a pain he was! He waited for everyone that was at the house to get dressed in their gowns and tuxedos, then started taking pictures. "Stand over here, stand over there, stand this way," he said. Make up your mind already! Everyone wanted me to be in some of the photos, but I didn't want any part of it. For one thing, I had just found out that I, Bruce, the protector and guardian of the family, had NOT even been invited to the ceremony! I was so mad, so disappointed and hurt, you have no idea! I wanted to bite someone, but didn't know who to nip. So I started growling at the photographer, and was told to keep quiet. The fact that I was not invited to the wedding really steamed me. You have a Best Man, Maid of Honor, Flower Girl, and Ring Bearer; why can't you have a Best Dog? I won't bite anyone, I promise! But nobody wanted to listen to me.

Just before Cornelia walked out of the house for the last time as a single woman, she picked me up and had a sort of heart-to-heart talk with me. She told me that she loved me and that everything was going to be all right. She said she was not going to leave me completely. I tried to give her a kiss, but had I done that, I would have ruined her make-up. And with that, everyone left the house for the evening. I never felt so lonely in that house as I did that night. I was actually crying; crying tears of loneliness.

It was many hours later when Ted and Ourania came back home. They told me it was a beautiful wedding and that everyone had a great time at the reception. They also said that I was a good dog. Good dog, indeed! There I was, lonely and heartsick, and all they could say to me was that I was a good dog! Well, bah humbug to you! For the first time ever, I was actually planning on running away

21

from home. But then I was thinking, *Now where could I possibly go at that hour of the night?* I then decided to stay at the house for a few more days and see what would happen.

One thing I had forgotten to mention; Nick and Dena came up from Florida to be there at Cornelia's wedding as part of the wedding party. They stayed for a few days at Dena's parents' home on Staten Island after the wedding, then went back home to Florida.

Until the house was sold completely, the remaining members of the household had decided that I was to sleep downstairs with Constantine and Amanda, and that Constantine was going to take me for walks when he was home; if not, that responsibility fell on Ted's shoulders. I must admit, however, I miss not having Cornelia walk with me. When we used to walk together, we would run together, I would chew on the leash, we would sit on the bench together and look at all the other people looking at us. With Ted walking me, it's walk, then sit on the bench, then walk back home. I realize Ted is an older gentleman, but I'm a spring chicken, and I need to roam around and bark at people and pretend to bite them. It's fun making people, total strangers, look at you with weird or alarmed expressions on their faces. Keeps them off balance, so to speak.

Well, it wasn't long after Cornelia's wedding that Ted and Ourania finally sold the house and everyone that was left was starting to pack their possessions. I myself had very little to pack; just my bowls, my puppy chow and whatever toys I had. I spent most of my time watching everyone else pack up their things. Let me just say, you humans accumulate an awful lot of stuff. You save this, you save that, then you forget what it was you saved or why you saved it. Then, the items you saved become forgotten and never seen again until you decide to move. And when that happens, a "trip down memory lane" usually occurs. Then, an even more difficult decision comes up; save it again and take it with you, or throw it away. And based on what I've seen, just about half the stuff you saved, then forgot about, then re-found because you are moving, gets thrown out the second time around. Weird, no?

It took days for Ted and Ourania and Constantine and Amanda to sort through all the things they had in that house and decide to keep and put them in boxes. An awful lot of stuff was thrown out. For Ted and Ourania, a lot of memories, both good and bad, resurfaced while they went through their belongings. And when moving day finally came, there was a new beginning for all the members of the family, and all that was left was a house, with memories, both good and bad, of its own.

Ted and Ourania had moved to a retirement community somewhere in Toms River, New Jersey. Constantine and Amanda were fortunate to find an apartment in the same complex as Cornelia and John. While Cornelia's apartment was nice, Constantine's was much bigger and roomier. There were two floors to his apartment; the downstairs where the entrance was and the living room; and upstairs, where the kitchen, dining area and the bedroom were. There was even a small patio area where you could hang out when the weather was nice. Cornelia's apartment was on one floor and had a storage attic. While the street that the complex was located on was busy, the neighborhood itself was quiet. I was a little confused and dazed after moving from Brooklyn to Staten Island, but after a while I felt right at home living in a more peaceful community. When either Constantine or Amanda were home, they took care of me. If not, then Cornelia and/or John would come over and take care of me. It really felt nice, being waited on by four people. And I didn't have to even snap my paws, either. Just give them the old, sad puppy-dog look, and they come running. Pretty neat, eh? But it felt so good to be reunited with Cornelia, even though we are a few doors apart from each other. At least we were not as far apart as we had been for the past few months.

John had a job working in Midtown Manhattan. Constantine worked in Brooklyn at first, then he started to work on Staten Island. Amanda was still going to college full-time, and working part-time. And Cornelia was working part-time at the GAP on Staten Island. So all four people really didn't see much of each other during the week. But I would mostly be in Constantine's apartment guarding the place when no one was home. Then after everyone came home, I could relax and unwind while Constantine and Amanda cooked and ate dinner, straightened out the apartment, fed me, then took me out for a walk.

But being at home all by myself during the week has its drawbacks, too. For one thing, if there wasn't anything going on, I would get bored very easily. I didn't want to sleep all day, otherwise people would think I was sick, or dead, or even worse, people might start to think I'm not a dog, but a cat! When I'm by myself and fresh and alert, I gotta do something! The hunter in me dictates that I look for adventure, and not wait for adventure to come to me. After all, I'm three years old now in human life, I'm in the prime of my life, I'll pretend this and pretend that; what could possibly go wrong?

Sometimes I would hear strange noises in the apartment, so I would go and investigate. If the noise was coming from the bathroom, I would go in there and try to determine its cause. And then I would be lured in by a scent coming from the small garbage can that was there, and see what item inside the can was that smelled so good (or bad). I would somehow lay the can down on its side and sort through it, like a true detective. Then, in the midst of my search, I would be attacked from behind by the toilet paper dispenser. I would fight back by grabbing its tail and drag it out into either the bedroom or into Constantine's study area. When the toilet paper monster would not fight back, I knew I had conquered it, and would leave it where it was for Constantine and Amanda to see, and reward me for my brave and heroic deed. For some strange reason, they were not happy to see the toilet paper monster dead and laying all over the place. Here I am, trying to protect the both of them from some unforeseen demonic and potential danger, and they're not happy about it. I guess the next time I take care of these demons, I have to somehow dispense of them quietly outside the apartment and pretend nothing happened.

Sometimes, when I am not patrolling the apartment, I may look around for something out of the ordinary to eat, rather than just munch on my plain old dog food. Doing this, I know, will get me into trouble, but I need to come up with a foolproof plan to fetch some delicious human food and not get into trouble. And there were times when either Constantine or Amanda would leave something on the dining room table, forget that it was there, then I would eat it, then they would somehow remember there was something they forgot, then go and look for it, then couldn't find it because I had just eaten it, then accuse one another of taking it, but would never blame me, because I would sit there quietly and never admit it. The trick here is to act fast and not look guilty. A lot of times I would act fast but somehow still look guilty and it was as if they were looking at me and reading my mind. So I learned to wait patiently enough for them to leave the apartment first, then I would look around.

One morning, after Constantine had gone off to work and Amanda went to school, I did my usual walkaround when I noticed something small on the livingroom table downstairs. I went over to it, sniffed it and I was like, "Wow, this smells good!" Just to be on the safe side, I made sure Constantine and Amanda were not around before I checked this item out. They weren't, so I walked over to the small object on the table, picked it up and went to work on it. And you know what it was? A small chocolate Hershey bar wrapped in a cute foil wrapper. Boy, was it good! It didn't take me long to eat it, either. It kinda almost melts in your mouth. I was like, "Are there any more of these things around?"

I was sure there were, so I started searching for them. It took me a while, but I found them; they were in a glass container on top of the counter in the kitchen upstairs. How did I find them, you ask? Well, I am a hunter, with an acute sense of smell, of course. Now that I've found them, my next problem was how to get at them. There were no chairs near the counter, and the counter was way too high for me to jump up to, so I had no other choice, I had to wait for either Constantine or Amanda to come home and give me more. In the meantime, I just had to be satisfied with my dreary-looking dog food. Oh, and in case you are wondering, it was Amanda who found the foil wrapper on the floor. I looked at her, she looked at me, and she laughed.

One thing I have not been able to figure is why you humans, especially those that have been together for a while, have to constantly argue, yell and scream at one another. I guess being an only dog has its advantages. For one thing, I don't have to get into an argument with another dog as to who has the better fur, or dog food, or why the Yankees are better than the Mets. Usually you humans argue over the silliest of things, and sometimes cause one person to leave. Now, I'm not going to get into any specifics here, but Amanda has left Constantine more than once. And every time she left, my heart sank. Amanda did have friends on Staten Island she could stay with in case she and Constantine would have a bad argument. Finally, one day, Amanda had had enough, wrote Constantine a good-bye note, gave me a long and tearful kiss, and walked away, never to return. Constantine had spoken to her since, asking her to come back, and she refused. Since then, Constantine had been going out on dates, and even brought them to the apartment to see me, but while they were all very nice, they just were not as warm as Amanda was. I really missed her.

It was around this time that Cornelia and John were going about their business of trying to start a family. During their stay at the apartment, and they eventually stayed there a little more than four years, Cornelia had gotten pregnant three times; only to have two miscarriages and an ectopic pregnancy. Both Cornelia and John were distraught that these incidents happened; especially Cornelia. So, to cheer her up, Constantine would bring me over to her place to give her some TLC (Tender Loving Canine-care). And I knew just what to do, too. All I had to do was lay as close to Cornelia as I possibly could, so she could pet me and cuddle me so much as to ease her mind over the miscarriages. That was my way of cheering her up, by letting her take care of me. And this is coming from a dog who didn't spend one day in grade school. Who says we dogs are dumb?

There were times when Cornelia was home by herself

during the week while Constantine and John were at work, so she would come to Constantine's apartment and bring me to her place. Because her apartment faced the main street, I would lay on the chair that was under a window and look out and see what was going on. I would see a lot of cars going back and forth, just like on Foster Avenue in Brooklyn. But I knew this was a much quieter neighborhood. I really felt at ease there. Cornelia would take me for a nice long walk around the area, and no one would bother us. And when I'm in Cornelia's apartment, I would look out the window, watching all the people walk by, bark at the mailman when he came by, be happy with glee when John came home, and watch the rain and snow when they fell. It was really a nice spot to sit and watch the world go by.

Usually, when someone came home or someone else that I know would come for a visit, I would greet them with a few barks and then I would shower them with affection by letting them pick me up and I would give them a lot of kisses. For all you humans that still do not understand our canine way of life, that is our way of welcoming you to our home or place of residence, so please accept our hospitality, make yourself at home, but don't make a mess of the place, because I do not forget who is messy and who is not.

Some of you humans believe that our "kissing" you is a sign that we adore you. That is partially true; but sometimes when I "kiss" someone, I am actually tasting and smelling whatever food crumbs or sauce you have all over your mouth. I just want to know why you humans are eating something so good while I have to be content with dog food. But a lot of times, I am expressing my true love for you. Then, you humans want to know why we dogs are so sloppy when we "kiss" you. Let me explain that in this way: John's brother had a beagle named Sparky. Sparky was a dog who had a philosophy of life that, if you summarized it in a nutshell, it would come down to this; "Easy come, easy go," meaning, whatever happens, happens. But he also believed a kiss to a human should be affectionate, and a lot of it. Anything less simply will not do. Sparky's philosophy of kissing is this: "If it ain't wet and sloppy, it ain't a kiss!"

Cornelia's husband, John, is a nice guy, and I like him, but sometimes he can be one strange dude. One Saturday morning, Constantine, who was working at the Home Depot store in Staten Island, had to go to work. So I was laying down on his bed in the upstairs bedroom. There I was laying there nice and comfortably, daydreaming of Mariah Carey, when all of a sudden I heard a noise coming from downstairs. At first I thought it was coming from outside, so I stayed where I was. Then I heard another noise, and then another noise. So I growled and let loose a soft bark. We dogs use this "soft" bark to warn any intruder that there is a dog inside the premises. (If you believe that, you'll believe anything.) Anyhow, I kept on hearing noises coming from downstairs. So I started barking loudly.

Normally, an intruder hearing any dog barking is

supposed to be running away from the area, but these noises kept coming closer to me. Then I heard what sounded like footsteps walking up the stairs, so I barked even louder and more furiously, and still the noises were coming closer! I was like, "Oh no, what do I do now?"

So I jumped off the bed, but stayed in the bedroom. The footsteps were coming even closer toward me. I'm barking like crazy, and then I see a shadow coming toward the room. Now I'm thinking two things: *Who is the intruder, and why is he or she not running away from my barking?* I thought, *Where is Underdog when you need him?* Both the shadow and the footsteps were coming even closer. Now, I'm getting frantic, barking as much as I could. I see the shadow's arm rise, and I'm thinking, *This is it! Dog Heaven, here I come!* The shadow ran toward me and growled, and I jumped and panicked and . . . it's John! He came over to deliberately scare me! I was like, you dirty, four-eyed rat fink, you! He saw that I was scared and laughed. That was not funny, you four-eyed punk! He picked me up and apologized for giving me such a fright. Good thing for him that he apologized, otherwise I would have bitten him in the you-know-where. But then I calmed down and realized that if I had bitten him, I probably would have been arrested for child abuse.

One thing I have never been able to feel comfortable with is being in a car. And I don't know why. I was never too comfortable being on an airplane, either. I guess I would rather be in a stationary dwelling such as a house, rather than be in something that moves, such as a car. I feel rather safe in a house because there is no trembling motion as there would be in a car. That's one reason. Another reason is that when I am in a car, anyone's car, the person driving the car is taking me someplace, and I do have a fear that if I go to another place, I would not come back home. Maybe the person is taking me to the veterinarian's, or dog quack's office, or to the dog pound, or to the woods to leave me there. You humans tell me you are taking me to Toms River to visit your parents, but how do I know that for sure?

Once I'm in the car, I am fine, until you turn on the engine and the car moves. Then my heart starts racing, my pulse quickens, my paws get all sweaty, I start panting more heavily more heavily, and I'm ready to either throw up or go to the bathroom in the car. You humans tell me to calm down and relax. How can I relax when I am very suspicious as to where you could be taking me? But most of the time, you are taking me someplace other than the vet's office. And once I get there, I begin to relax and be myself and try to have a good time. A lot of dogs can relax in a car; I can't. I was a nervous wreck in Constantine's car when we moved from Brooklyn to Staten Island. Constantine kept on telling me to relax, but that was like telling a hungry lion not to eat meat.

I can remember going to Nick's house in Florida by being sedated on an airplane, but on one of those trips, Ted decided he wanted to drive all the way back from Florida to Brooklyn. I don't quite remember the reason for that, but I do remember Ted driving Ourania,

Cornelia and myself back to Brooklyn. What a trip that was! I had to sit in the back seat with Cornelia, and everyone was trying to get me to calm down, but I couldn't. I was huffing and puffing and panting and driving everyone crazy. Hell, I was driving myself crazy! We stopped every few hours to stretch our legs, and go to the bathroom. Of course, I could only go potty outside a facility, and not inside. And every time we stopped to get something to eat, two of them would go inside to eat, while one person would stay in the car with me. When one person finished eating, that person would come out and the other would go in and eat. They did this so I wouldn't be alone in the car. I guess they didn't want anyone else to kidnap, or dog-nap, me and hold me for ransom. And when we stopped at a roadside inn to spend the night, I was told to be a good dog and not bark or cry, otherwise, we would all have to spend the night sleeping in the car.

Ourania sneaked me in under her jacket, while Ted and Cornelia went to the front desk. Now, let the truth be told here; or at least my version of the truth anyway. I tried to be as quiet as I could, but I kept hearing strange noises coming from the other rooms, and since it was my duty to protect my masters from harm, I barked to warn any strangers that I am here and if anyone were to come near my masters, they would have to deal with me first. Hey, it must have worked, because no one dared to come near us. But, to make a long story short, we spent the entire night at the inn, left there early the next day, stopped along the way to stretch and grab a bite to eat. When we finally arrived home, we were all exhausted, myself included, between not being comfortable in the car, and worrying if anything was going to happen to my masters during the ride home. It was a long ride, and everyone had done their part to make the journey safe for everyone else; myself included, of course.

Anyway, living in the two apartments in the same complex was working out well. Even though I didn't mind being by myself for a while, on any given day I was with either Constantine or with Cornelia and John. I was never totally alone, and that felt good. There were times when Constantine would put the leash on me to take me for a walk and we would end up going to Cornelia's place. Or Constantine would trust me enough to just simply open his door and I would automatically go to Cornelia's. But there were also times when Constantine would open his door and I would just go about doing my business outside and then decide to go for a little walk by myself. That, Constantine didn't like; nor did Cornelia for that matter. All I was doing was exploring my new surroundings on Staten Island by myself. I was going to come back, honestly; that is, if I didn't chase a car on the busy street first, or run after anyone that looked suspicious, or get into an argument with another dog. Seriously, I was going to come back, but no one seemed to trust me. I must admit, though, it was kind of fun watching Constantine chase after me when he realized my true intentions. Then, he would get all mad at me and call me a bad dog. Hey, you only live once. You gotta have a little fun once in a while.

There are times, however, when I do feel lonely when no one else is at home. Hell, I even feel lonely when some-one is home. When anyone is home, I just get into a play-ful mood and try to get them to chase me around the apartment. The trouble is, sometimes when I want to play, everyone else is either tired or just not in the mood. When that happens, I let out another one of my "soft" barks to attract attention and then dare them to chase me. Someone would either chase after me, or I would be told to keep quiet. Even when Constantine has his friends over, I try to attract attention to me so I don't feel so lonely. I realize that is the ham in me, but being an only dog on this side of the family, I like to be pampered and spoiled. (Now, that's the brat in me.) But every time I do make a commotion, I am being told to shut up. Then I do the next best thing; act like a little angel and put on my cute puppy-dog face and wait for someone to notice me. Then, when someone does see me, I pretend to "play" with them, by having them throw my toys so I can fetch them. That way, I can attract attention toward me. That's the ham in me again. And then I would sit patiently by the snack table and wait for someone to give me a little sam-pling of the hors d'oeuvres. I even do this at Cornelia's place when she and John have guests, too. But a lot of times, when I am at Cornelia's place, and she and John are expecting company, one of them would escort me back to Constantine's place and leave me there until their guests leave.

It's a funny thing, but I often wonder what my masters think of what I am doing when I'm alone. I mean, do they think I am indeed watching over their house while they are gone, or do they like to think that I am inviting some of my friends over for a little get-together, or even having a little party? Believe me, I would love to have a small party with a few friends. But I can't call up my pals on the telephone and "woof" them to come over. For one thing, my paws would mess up the push buttons on the phone. Another thing would be that my masters would always come back home at the most inconvenient time and catch me doing something that I am not supposed to be doing, like licking a girl dog. With my luck, I would get caught doing something like that. So when I think of the worst case scenarios that could happen, that's when I decide to play it cool and not have anyone over. It's much safer that way.

Constantine's apartment is plenty big enough to have a small party with friends and family. There were plenty of times when Cornelia's parents and Nick and Dena and Cornelia's oldest brother, Gregory, and his family would come for a little get-together and would wind up going back and forth between Cornelia's place and Constantine's apartment. Everything worked out well in that aspect. Family get-togethers such as these were always happy times for me, because I would always be around the people I was raised with and would have fun with them. Gregory and his family lived in New Jersey, and it was right about this time that Cornelia and John started to do some house hunting for themselves in New

Jersey. They both decided that Staten Island was getting too crowded and the price of houses there was too high, so the first town they looked at was Sayreville, New Jersey. Now, keep in mind that while those two would-be home-owners were checking out some less expensive real estate to live in, I was guarding Constantine's apartment. Nobody ever invited me to help check out these places and value my opinion on where to move to, so I kept my trap shut. Cornelia and John said they found a nice house in Sayreville, but after considering all the financial difficulties they would have, they decided to wait another year. This way, they would plan their finances better in the hopes of finding a better home. And that was good news for me. After all, I was getting very comfortable living between those two apartments. I wouldn't want Cornelia to move away from me again, like she did when she first got married. I felt lonely then, and did not want to feel that way again anytime soon.

Meanwhile Nick and Dena had sold their house in Florida and moved to Staten Island. They were living in a house that was in the custody of Dena's parents. Their house was only about twenty minutes away by car from the apartment complex. Nick and Dena loved living in Florida, but they were too far away from everyone else, and wanted to move back north. They had brought with them from Florida a small, white Maltese dog which they named Rocky. Don't be fooled by his tough-sounding name. Rocky is a quiet homebody compared to me, an aggressive go-getter. When I first met Rocky, I was like,

"This kid's got a long way to go." He was too quiet and too shy. I saw right away that I would have my hands full trying to teach him the facts of life.

Anyway, now that Nick and Dena were living on Staten Island, all of us on Cornelia's side of the family got together more often during the holidays and for birthdays. And that's the way a family should be; together, and no one is off on their own. Besides, whenever the family did get together at the apartment complex, everyone would be happy to see me and would spoil me by generously giving me some scraps. I never went to bed hungry after those get-togethers, let me tell you!

Cornelia and John waited almost a year before they started to look around again for a house. After a few months, they announced that they had found a cute little house in Keansburg, New Jersey. Turns out, this place was just a few minutes away from where Gregory and his family were living. So then, Cornelia and John went through the paperwork process that it takes to try to buy a house, and I was like, "I hope this does not go through." I would be devastated if Cornelia moved away from me again. But lo and behold, they were approved for their mortgage and started to pack up their things to move into their new home. I was thinking, *This is all just another bad dream and could not possibly be true.* I was waiting for someone to pinch me so I could wake up from this nightmare.

But nobody pinched me and reality set in one hot August day in 1999, when a moving truck pulled into the apartment parking lot and stopped at Cornelia's door. I watched in absolute horror as three guys loaded up their truck with Cornelia and John's furnishings that morning. After the truck was loaded, Cornelia and John came over to Constantine's apartment and told me they would be back the next day to take more of their stuff to bring to their new home. I was completely saddened by everything that was going on. I thought, *Cornelia, you're leaving me, again? How could you do this to me?*

Constantine was off from work that week to help Cornelia and John move to Keansburg. That first day, the movers did everything, so there wasn't much anyone else could do but welcome Cornelia and John to their new home. Cornelia's parents came up from Toms River to see the place and then the four of them were going out for dinner. The next day, I went with Constantine to check it out. It was really a nice house, everything on one floor with three bedrooms, one bathroom, one living room, the kitchen, a dining area and a small foyer for the washer and dryer, as well as the hot water heater. There is an unfinished attic for Cornelia and John to store their junk. There is a fenced-in backyard for kids and myself to play in. They also have a front lawn, but that area did not have a fence protecting it. The colors of the house were nice too; a brown roof with tan-colored siding around the house. I was really impressed! Constantine volunteered himself to paint all the rooms inside the house over time. John had taken off that week to help with the move and unpack the boxes and help organize the house the way Cornelia wanted it. Husbands usually have no say in this, I learned.

Cornelia and John still had to go back and forth from Staten Island to New Jersey to get more of their stuff from Constantine's place. The last time Cornelia came to the apartment to get the last of her possessions, she looked at me, picked me up and told me not to worry about anything, that Constantine was going to take good care of me and that we would see each other again soon. And with that, she and John drove off in their car to go back to their new home, where Constantine was hard at work painting their living room.

If I ever really felt truly alone, this was it; Cornelia and John now live in another state, along with Gregory and his family, and her parents. Constantine would either be at work, or out with his friends. For the very first time, there was only one member of my original adoptive family living within ten miles, and that was Constantine. I really felt lonely and scared. Constantine was the only person to take care of me now; he fed me, walked me and kept me company. These were times when I wished I was not the only dog in the family.

If I thought that was bad, the worst was yet to come. A new landlord took over the apartment complex a few months prior and decided to raise the rent. Constantine then took it upon himself to look around for a smaller place to live, and he found it, still on Staten Island, in a not-so-hot neighborhood. He rented a much smaller apartment on a quiet street only blocks from where John grew up. After living in a big house in Brooklyn, then moving to a decent-sized apartment in Staten Island, and then moving into a place I would almost qualify as a studio apartment, I was thinking, *What next? A cage in a kennel? Can't get any lower than that, or can it?*

Constantine's newer apartment was so small, he had to leave some of his furnishings behind in the other apartment, then gave some other things to his parents. Moving to this place was a HUGE adjustment to the both of us. The neighborhood was so different, and when I had to go to the bathroom at night, Constantine had to get up and walk with me outside the apartment. There was no patio area where I could walk and do my thing, as I did in the other place. And the hallways . . . the echoes you would hear! You always had to talk softly, or in my case, bark softly, so you wouldn't cause a commotion in the complex. I just did not feel right there, just didn't feel safe. At least, whenever Constantine left me by myself at the other place, I felt safe, even though I was alone, but not so here. I didn't feel safe at all. And even though the neighbors seemed friendly, I was constantly hearing noises everyday, at all hours of the day. I was hoping Constantine would move back to the other apartment complex, or move to a safer environment, but with him being by himself now, the odds of us moving again anytime soon were very slim.

When Nick and Dena saw the new apartment, they were flabbergasted. Nick did not approve of the place at all, and he told Constantine that he did not think that

Constantine nor I would be safe there. Constantine told Nick that the place was only temporary and that he was going to look around for a better place soon. He even told Cornelia and John the same thing when they came to see the place, and even to his parents. But I knew better. Less expensive apartments don't grow on trees, and Constantine could not afford for us to move any-time soon. So I just had to relax, keep cool, and wait . . . and try not to be scared of my newer surround-ings, even though there were times I would be scared silly just going out for walks.

My being alone almost eleven hours a day while Constantine went off to work, and constantly hearing strange noises in the building, and not being able to go outside to go to the bathroom finally took its toll on me. I eventually went to the bathroom on his new rugs and car-pets. And I think Constantine was starting to realize him-self that I didn't want to be in that place, so he sat me down and told me he would like me to live with Cornelia and John. "They have a house," he said. And they have a yard where I could run around and go to the bathroom anytime I wanted. A great portion of their yard was fenced in (only the front lawn was not yet fenced in), and I would be together with Cornelia again once more. And Constantine asked me if I wanted that. That's like asking a millionaire if he wants another million. I looked at him with my happy, puppy-dog look, smiled, and gave him a kiss, saying "Yes!! Get me out of this hellhole!" And with that, Constantine made arrangements with Cornelia for me to stay with her and John permanently starting the end of the first December that they bought their nice house.

It seemed like an eternity, but the day finally arrived that I would move in with Cornelia and John. John was at work, so Constantine brought me to their house and cried a little, saying I would be better off at Cornelia's house than inside a small apartment. Constantine left Cornelia with some of my toys, my dog food, and my identification papers. Hey, we animals have to have some I.D. too, you know. I couldn't help but think; there I was, seven years old, I was born and raised in Brooklyn, then moved to a nice apartment on Staten Island, then moved to a much smaller apartment, still on Staten Island; now I am living in Cornelia's house in New Jersey. Kinda makes my head spin a little, going all over the place like that.

Constantine didn't stay at the house long; he had some things to do. But before he left, he told me to be a good boy for "sister and brother-in-law." *Brother-in-law?* You mean, John, that four-eyed dude is my brother-in-law? Heavens to Betsy!! Okay, I might as well go along with this charade, as long as it keeps everyone happy.

It didn't take me long to get used to living in New Jersey, just as long as Cornelia was with me. All I had to do was go the bathroom in their backyard. Believe me, it was a helluva lot easier to do it this way than to have Constantine walk me outside his apartment. All I do now is stand by the sliding door in the back, then either

Cornelia or John would open the door, and let me out. No putting on the leash, no more walking down the street, checking out everyone else's front lawns, and no more attacking strangers walking on the opposite side. Yes, a dog can get pretty spoiled doing things this way!

But that's not the only way I can have things to my advantage. I even have old brother-in-law John feeding me scraps off his dinner plate! How about that? Now I can sample Cornelia's meats and beefs and fish, and still have my (ugh!) dog food. But as much as I miss not being with Constantine, I am getting the good old red carpet treatment in my new habitat. All I hope is that Constantine gets a better place to live, not just for me, but for himself as well. He deserves a better place.

Cornelia is not working, so we are constantly together, day and night. What more can I ask for? I even sleep on their bed with them at night. Let me tell you something about this though; that John, MAN, can he snore! I always thought Cornelia was bad enough with her tossing and turning, but now I have to put up with the snoring, as well! It's a miracle I get any sleep at night. And then Cornelia and John have the nerve to ask me why I sometimes take a nap during the day. Well, one reason is to make sure those two are safe and sound while they sleep, and the other reason is the noise they make and their tossing and turning. I said it before, and I'll say it again: it's not easy being a dog!

When Cornelia and John first moved to Keansburg, they had no idea just how many children there were in the neighborhood. On Halloween day of the first year they were there they sure found out. On that year, Halloween fell on a Sunday, and I found out later on that Sunday was a beautiful day, with pleasant temperatures. All the little kids were out trick-or-treating. In less than one hour, Cornelia and John went through ten full bags of candy. Then John had to go out and buy a few more bags. They, too, were gone in a flash. It got so bad that Cornelia and John had no choice but to leave the house for a little while. They came back when it started to get dark. All I have to say is that I was glad I was not there that day. I would have gone crazy barking at all those kids, telling them to leave my masters alone.

Besides there being a lot of kids in Keansburg, there were also a lot of dogs there. And there were a lot of dogs that roamed around the neighborhood without their masters walking them. So, when I moved there, I knew I was in for a lot of competition. Cornelia and John didn't feel right to put me out toward the back of their house, because they knew how inquisitive I was (and still am) and might somehow venture through the fences they have on the sides of their house and explore the front lawn. Since the front lawn was not protected by a fence, the neighborhood dogs, and kids, for that matter could walk on their lawn. And the dogs, well, when you gotta go, you gotta go! And I would sit on the ottoman facing the front of the house and bark at them, telling them to go to the bathroom on THEIR front lawns! Needless to say, those dogs didn't want to listen to me and you know what happened.

So, to take care of that problem, Cornelia and John decided it would be wise to get a fence for the front lawn. This way, they could keep me on their property and keep everyone else out. They made an appointment with someone to come and install a fifty-foot metal fence in front of the house and take out one of the side fences. So one day, while John was at work, someone came and did just that and let me tell you, the fence in the front looked nice. Now, Cornelia and John can let me out the front entrance and I can do my business all around their house. I can now stand on my masters' front lawn and let other people have a piece of my mind without worrying if they would retaliate. What a wonderful feeling that is!

It really felt great to be able to sit outside on the front lawn on a nice day, knowing there was a fence in place, and you could sit out there and watch the world go by. I really felt safe with the entire outside of their house being fenced in. But having a fence around the front lawn does not always guarantee instant security. Strangers do come and open the front gate to come to the house. And when that happens, either John or Cornelia have to restrain me from giving them a piece of my mind. And then there was Rocco.

One day, I'm sitting on the front lawn, minding my own business, and a Great Dane walked by. He looked at me and I looked at him. He said his name was Rocco and asked me if I could come out and play with him. I told him I couldn't leave my master alone, so Rocco said O.K., he would come into the front lawn to play. I said, "Okay." He then walked over to the next door neighbor's front steps, stood on the top step and leaped over the fence onto our front lawn. I was like, "Wow! That was great, Rocco. Now we can play together."

So, we started running back and forth along the side of the house. We were really having a good time together when Cornelia came out and freaked out when she saw Rocco. She kept yelling at me to come into the house. I asked Rocco if he would like to stay awhile and meet my masters. He told me he couldn't, that it was time for him to leave. And with that, he walked back a few paces, then ran toward the fence and leaped over onto the sidewalk. He looked at me, and I barked a farewell to him, and then he walked away. Cornelia was screaming at me to come into the house. She started calling me a bad dog. Me? A bad dog? For what? For playing on the front lawn with a Great Dane? He was only with me for a few minutes, and then he left. Rocco was lonely, and wanted someone to play with him. That was all. No need to panic. Never fear, I'm here. Just because I'm a dog doesn't mean I can't enjoy a few moments with someone of my own kind, now does it?

Sometimes, when I'm outside sitting on the front steps or sitting on the ottoman in the living room, I look straight ahead at this big oak tree directly across the street from my masters' house. I look at it and I sometimes wonder what it must feel like to be like that big oak tree. I wonder who planted it, how old it is, how many times the leaves have grown on it in the spring, and how many times they have fallen in the autumn seasons. I wonder how many summers the tree has seen, now many people have walked past it day after day, and how many different families have lived in the house that tree is next to. I wonder how many squirrels have climbed its arching branches, how many birds have rested on those same branches after flying around the neighborhood, how many stray cats have gotten stuck up there, how many dogs have gone to the bathroom on the tree's base. I wonder how many autumns there have been in which that tree's leaves have fallen onto my master's front lawn, enticing John to go out and rake them up. Yes, I wonder all of that and more. And I even wonder why, in spite of mankind's great intelligence and inventions and ingenuity, you humans still do not appreciate nature's gifts any more than we other animals do. I can't speak for the other animals, but we dogs really enjoy all the natural gifts Mother Nature gives us, except, of course, for the cold weather and the rain and snow.

By now, John and Cornelia were starting to call me that certain nickname "Boopie". It was John who first thought of it, and Cornelia thought it was so cute, so then *she* started calling me "Boopie". Before this, people were calling me by my real first name, which was "Bruce," and then "Budgie" which is what Constantine still calls me by. Sometimes John gets a little carried away with "Boopie" that he has called me "Poopie" and even refers me to be his "little Poopie-dog". Is that low, or what? I have never been so insulted in all my dog years! But even Cornelia's niece, Christina, has been calling me "Boopie" as well. I'll go along with this crazy name thing for now, until I get so sick of hearing that name I'll throw up on John's bed pillow. Cornelia has even gone so far as to call me "Mr. Magoo" after the cartoon character. "Mr. Magoo"!?! I'm like, "Now where in the name of Lassie did she come up with that nickname? I mean, 'Boopie' is bad enough, but 'Mr. Magoo'!?! C'mon!" Sometimes, John would even call me "Puppy". Now, I like it when he and Cornelia call me that. It kind of makes me feel young and vibrant again.

I remember when John first came into the picture, he was driving a two-door blue Pontiac LeMans. He had that car for a long time. He first met Cornelia with that car, they dated with that car, they got married with that car, lived and traveled on Staten Island for four years with that car, went to the Poconos with that car, bought a house in Keansburg with that car, moved to New Jersey with that car; let's face it, they did a lot with that car. It was all just a matter of time before that Pontiac started to fall apart. John always tried to take good care of it, taking it for tune-ups and stuff. But then the brakes started to go. They have been serviced before, but it go to the point where Cornelia and John would take the car to the mechanic's garage almost every two months for the same thing. So finally, they decided to buy a brand new car.

One Saturday morning, they went to a Nissan dealer just to look at new cars. It was a good three hours before they returned. And of course, I had to go to the bathroom. So as soon as they came back, they opened the front door and I didn't even bother to say "Hi" to them. I just went out onto the front lawn and did my thing. Then I looked out onto the street, expecting to see the blue Pontiac. Instead, I saw a tan-colored Nissan Sentra; brand-spanking new. I was like, "Wow! Where did this come from? Did you guys lease this thing, or what?" I had to do a double-take when I first saw it. It was beautiful! And with four doors, too. It's too bad I don't like car rides; otherwise, I would ask to go out for a spin. But that's okay. I know eventually I will be going for more than just a few rides in this new car.

One thing Cornelia and John did during the very first Christmas they spent in Keansburg was put their decorated tree in the front window where the ottoman usually is. When I went to live with them almost a year later, and saw that they were going to put that tree in that same spot, I protested. I looked at them and tried to make them understand that I needed that spot by the front window to be able to check out what was going on outside their house. With that tree being there, there was no way I could fulfill my obligation as a security guard. Since neither one of them understood dog-talk (and you humans think you are so smart), I had no choice but to do something very drastic: I almost went to the bathroom on the Christmas tree! So, what do you think happened? I got yelled at, which is nothing new, but I made hinting gestures that I would do it again if they didn't wake up, smell the Starbucks coffee, and move that tree.

Finally, a miracle happened! Cornelia and John realized that they couldn't tangle with me over this issue and decided to move the tree to the far corner of the living room, in between the couch and the chair. And they even left the ottoman under the front window so I could sit there and fulfill my duty. That ottoman now stays in that spot 365 days a year, thanks to me! Now, Cornelia and John are a little leery about leaving the tree in the far corner unprotected from me, so they put the end table in front of the tree and leave it there when they are not in the living room for long periods of time. "Hey, guys!" I'm trying to say to them. "You don't have to do that! All I wanted you to do was move the tree away from the window! Even after all these years, don't you guys trust me?" I guess not.

As I have said before, Cornelia and John have a nice house. Of course, no one homeowner is ever satisfied with everything in a house, so there are a few changes that Cornelia and John are doing to their house, as well. I don't mean to brag, but I have been influential in helping them in that department. After all, they did get a new fence put on the front lawn, didn't they?

Another thing they have done was change the floor in their dining area and in their hallway. Previously, they had a hardwood floor in their dining area and an area rug was placed under their dining table. The area rug was nice, but the hardwood floor was a little worn. The floor in the hallway was covered by a carpet that stretched out to the living room and the three bedrooms. Cornelia and John hired someone to take out the carpet in the hallway and cover that floor and the floor in the dining room with a wood-like tile called Pergo. It took two men a few hours to lay it all down, and when they were finished, the floor looked awesome! It even looked like a real hardwood floor. Now, you're probably wondering if I had anything to do with this, right? Well, in a small way, I did. While Cornelia and John were out of the house for hours at a time, and sometimes I had to go to the bathroom, but couldn't leave the house, I had no real choice, so I went on the area rug and/or the carpet in the hallway. Of course, I got yelled at for that, but hey, when you gotta go, you gotta go. You know? Now that the hallway floor was covered with the Pergo tiles, I couldn't do anything on there so I continued to use the area rug as my bait. But that lasted only about another year.

You see, Cornelia's oldest brother, Gregory, got a new job. He was a manager for that coffee house called Starbucks. Because Cornelia's family was Greek, and everyone spoke Greek, Starbucks transferred Gregory and his family to Greece. This meant that Gregory had to sell his house in New Jersey and almost all of its furnishings. Cornelia had her eye on the dining room set that Gregory and Dorothy had, and asked if she could have it, and Gregory said she could. Less than two weeks before Gregory and Dorothy moved to Greece, the moving men showed up at Cornelia's house with the furniture. And when they placed that set in the dining room, the room itself looked great! Now, with the newer furniture in the dining room, Cornelia and John decided the room itself looked so great, they didn't put down the area rug. I was like, "Curses! There goes another of my favorite spots." So now, the only other room that I could do my thing on was the living room, and that was only if I had no way of getting outside of the house if my masters were not at home.

I had shamelessly used the living room carpet as my bathroom for a long while, almost as long as I have been living there, actually. The carpet itself was old to begin with; I guess, as old as the house. It was stained long before I came into the picture. So Cornelia and John were kind of fed up with how the carpet looked and smelled. John even used baking soda and water to help dissolve some stains and the smell, but that was a temporary thing. Sooner or later, the both of them knew they had to get a newer carpet.

So, just before New Year's 2004, they went to Home Depot and ordered a brand new carpet. It was a few days after New Year's that someone came to the house and measured the living room floor, then a few more weeks before two men came and installed the new carpet. And when they were done with that, the living room looked great. There were no more stains, and no more smells. And just to be on the safe side, Cornelia and John decided to lay down dropcloths around the general area where they believed I would go and make a few stains. But that didn't mean the new carpet would not be "christened" by me yet.

One day, while John was at work, Cornelia had gone out, and I really, really tried to wait for her to come back, honestly. But I couldn't help myself and piddled in the middle of the carpet. When Cornelia came home and saw what I had done, she was furious! She yelled at me and "threatened" to tell my "daddy" what I did. My "daddy" in this case was John. And sure enough, Cornelia went and told John what I had done. He yelled at me a little bit, but I tried to tell the both of them that I couldn't help it; I had to do it. Sorry, folks! Nature called, and when Nature calls, hardly anyone resists.

At this time, I am eleven and a half years old, in human years. In dog years, that is considered old. And Cornelia and John and everyone else are starting to wonder when I will begin to slow down a bit. In my case, you are as old as you feel. I may be old chronologically, but sometimes I feel as young as a puppy. I can still run around the coffee table in the living room. In fact, when John comes home at night from work, I try to tease him by getting him to chase me around that table a few times and then go under the bed in the bedroom. In my younger days, that was no problem. But now, when I do go under the bed, I have to stop and catch my breath before I can resume the chase. I find it fun and the activity does give me some exercise, but the real reason why I do it is to annoy John, because I know after a long and hard day at work, the last thing he wants to do is chase anyone around a table and under a bed. He almost never catches me, but he does wait for me to come out from under the bed to "scare" me, and when he does that, then he is getting even with me.

When you live with someone for as long as I have with Cornelia and John, you have a tendency to realize some of their quirky traits, or habits. In the past, I have gone through peoples' pocketbooks, closets, seeking out and eating whatever someone left on a table or on the floor, and then pretend that I was just an innocent by-stander, but almost all of the time, I would have been found out. Cornelia had a habit of pouring a glass of cold water for herself and would leave that glass of water all over the house. A lot of times, she would leave it on the coffee table in the living room. I would see it just sitting there, and I would say to myself, "That looks so refreshing!"

Almost every night, Cornelia and John would sit in the living room and watch T.V. Cornelia would be on the couch, with her glass of water on the coffee table, and John would sit on the chair. I would be sleeping instead of watching re-runs on TV-LAND. Every time Cornelia would move on the couch, I would wake up. And every time she would get up to go to the bathroom, I would get up, too, and pretend to stretch my legs. But I would almost always look to see if Cornelia left her glass of water on the table. If she did, I would get up and slowly (or rather, speedily) make my way toward the glass. That glass of cold water looked so much better than the water Cornelia and John put in my plastic bowl. The water in the glass looks so pure, so good; I just have to go at it.

If John is sitting on the couch, he would watch me. He would quietly tell me to get down, and at the same time, he would be laughing. But I would still make my way toward that glass, put my front paws on the table, reach over and then put my whole face INSIDE the glass and start licking that delicious water. And then . . . fireworks! Cornelia would walk in, see what I was doing, and yell out, "Bruce!!!!" Or, if she caught me getting close to the glass, she would yell, "Don't you dare!!" Then after a couple of seconds, she would let me drink some water out of her glass. The whole time this was going on, John was still sitting on the couch, laughing. I guess I must look cute doing this. But I don't care. I am thirsty, and I am not going to drink that warm water that is in my plastic bowl when I could have some cold, refreshing water straight out of a glass.

If my being picky and particular about drinking water is bad, my stubborn attitude for food is worse. After all, why should I have to eat my boring and bland dog food while you humans can eat almost anything you want. The foods you humans eat smells better and certainly tastes better. I must admit though, that even if my dog food is healthier for me to eat than your human food, the aromas of the foods you consume is just about second to none. While you humans eat real chicken, real meat, and real beef, I have to eat chicken-flavored dog food, meat flavor and beef flavor; I don't want anything flavored, I want the real thing!

When Cornelia cooks the meat or the poultries in her kitchen, my mouth waters for the real McCoy. But Cornelia won't share the stuff she cooks in her kitchen with me. So at night, during dinner time, I sit right at John's feet, and try to hypnotize him into giving me some samples. But a lot of times that doesn't work, so I just sit there and give him my sad-eyed puppy-dog look, and practically beg for him to share with me some of the food he is eating. And just like a fish, John takes the bait, and gives me scraps off his plate. He wouldn't hand me the scraps; I would end up nipping at his fingers. Instead, he would toss them to me, and I would catch them in mid-air and eat them. John would say that I catch better than the New York Mets. But he would almost always leave a scrap or two for me to have with my regular, boring dog food. Bless his heart, that sucker!

Then, it would be up to Cornelia to feed me my dinner with the tablescraps. But right after she finishes eating her dinner, she would relax for a moment or two and totally forget all about me. So, I always have to remind her that she has another mouth to feed. I would sit there next to her and let out some soft "woofs" and some growls, as if my stomach was growling. But I notice those soft woofs get to her, and she gets up mumbling something under her breath about what a "demanding little puppy" I am. Well, what do you want me to do? Go to bed hungry? In your dreams, sister! That'll be the day I go to bed with nothing in my stomach. Hey, we are all in this together. All three of us in this family have our own jobs to do, and all three of us should be properly compensated, however demanding or unreasonable we may be.

At night, when the three of us were getting ready to

go to bed, Cornelia and John would put me on the bed first, then they would climb into bed. In my younger days, I would be able to jump onto the bed unassisted. But lately, as I have gotten older, I find myself not being able to jump as high as before, so that's why Cornelia and/or John would pick me up and lay me on the bed. Usually, they would have me lay down in between them for a few moments, then they would start talking about this and that, and then bid the other good-night, pet me, and bid me good-night as well. At this point, I would get up from being in between them and walk to Cornelia's side. There are two reasons why I do this; one, because I am claustro-phobic, and do not want to be crushed if either Cornelia or John toss and turn and lay on top of me in their sleep. I deserve better than to be flattened out like a pancake by either one of these sleeping beauties. The other reason is, and I had mentioned this before, is that John snores and I don't need to hear that.

So, I would get up and go to Cornelia's side and lay there; nice and comfortably. (Besides, Cornelia smells better than John.) But because I am still the family secu-rity guard, I really don't get too much sleep at night. I lay awake on the bed just in case something happens. If I hear a strange noise and it is coming from outside of the house, I would growl, then bark. And I would keep on barking until I didn't hear that noise anymore. But in the process I would wake up both Cornelia and John, then John would get up and look out the windows in the front, then go into the kitchen and look out that window. Then he would come back into bed, say everything is all right, pet me, and tell me to go back to sleep. Little does he know that I sometimes tease him into thinking I actually did hear a noise and I would bark just to see what he would do.

But a lot of times I would have to get up in the middle of the night to go to the bathroom. When that happens and I can't wait any longer, I would get up, stand at the edge of the bed and "shake" myself, in such a way that either Cornelia or John would hear the chains on my collar rattle, wake up, see me standing at the edge of the bed, and know immediately that I have to go out. Then that one that wakes up would get up, carrying me off the bed, escort me to the front door, open it, let me out and wait for me. After a few private moments, I would come trotting up those front steps, be escorted back into the house and onto the bed. Then, that person goes back to bed, says "good-night" to me once again, and goes back to sleep. Then I'm happy that everyone else is happy that I went to the bathroom outside. I said it before, and I'll say it again: I really have Cornelia and John trained well.

During the work week, John is an early riser, and gets up before five A.M. I am always glad when he gets up because then I can go to sleep knowing that my tour of duty of guarding the house is over for that evening, John would usually go into the bathroom and shave, then take a shower. Then he would get dressed, and go to the store for his breakfast and the newspaper. He would then come back home, and have his breakfast while reading the newspaper.

Now, while he is doing all that, I am sound asleep, and I usually don't wake up until John is ready to go to work.

I would just lie there in bed, quietly; dozing off to LA-LA Land, when, all of a sudden, I would hear a familiar noise: the sound of a refrigerator door opening up, and that could mean only one thing; John is having dessert! He knows there is chocolate cake in the refrigerator, or a Scooter-Pie, so he is trying to help himself to the goodies. I'm like, "Wait a darn minute now, let me have some, too." I would get up and stand at the edge of the bed, and you know what happens then? John would come into the bedroom, pick me up, put me down on the floor and tell me to go to my bowl. So that's what I would do, hobble toward my bowl, and there it would be; a piece of chocolate cake or a piece of a Scooter Pie! I would be like, "Bless that sap's heart; he left me a treat!" And for him to let me eat in between meals, especially anything chocolate, makes John an O.K. guy in my book!

Now, usually on weekends, when John doesn't have to go to work, he'll sleep in a bit later. Then he would wake up around seven o'clock in the morning, see me laying on the bed and pet me. Then Cornelia would wake up a few minutes later and the two of them would pet me and say how cute I look lying in bed. They would put me in between them and turn me so my back would be on the bed and my stomach would be facing them. Cornelia would say to me, "Boopie! You like to expose yourself, eh?" Hey, it's not my idea to lie in your bed on my back. Then John would rub my stomach. I have to make sure he doesn't touch me anywhere else, or I'll really bite him. I really don't like to lay on my back for too long, because I suddenly get the urge to sneeze. And when I'm in their bed, and they lay me on my back, and I have to sneeze; well, I don't exactly give them too much of a warning. I either sneeze on them, or on their pillows. Either way, John laughs, and Cornelia yells at me. This routine had been going on for well over two years now; every time they lay me on my back, I get the urge, then I'll sneeze. Then, I'll get yelled at. You would think that after two years of the same old thing, they would learn not to have me in that position, but they'll keep on doing it. These humans. They do something they think is cute, then it backfires and they blame everyone but themselves. Typical.

A lot of times, Cornelia and John would be cuddling and petting me affectionately, then Cornelia would say something like, "What a good puppy we have!" and then John, being the comedian that he is, would sit up, look around, saying, "Where? Where?" And I would think, *Just this once, I would like to take a nibble out of him.*

Sometimes, if John is in a real playful mood, he would pick me up, hold me in his arm as if I were a baby, then gently swing me back and forth, singing, "Rock-a-bye, Boopie, on a tree-top," and I would look up at him, and say to myself, "This man's mind is gone!" When I look up at him, he would be looking at me, smiling, and I would be like, "Okay, I'm outta here," and I would try to squirm my way to get down by turning myself around in his arm, letting him know that playtime is over and I want to get down. Then John

61

would chuckle and say, "Alright, Squirmy. You wanna get down?" He would then put me down, and I would walk away from him, turning around to see if he was alright. And he would look back at me, smile and wave. Poor guy. I guess sometimes he has too much time on his hands and is in desperate need for a few more hobbies.

Normally, when John is on vacation, he usually takes one week at a time to either do some work around the house, or Cornelia and John would go away somewhere, just the two of them. (No dogs invited!) And usually when they do go away, Cornelia and John make arrangements for someone to take care of me and keep an eye on me (so I don't get into trouble). Sometimes that "someone" is Constantine. But there was a time in which Cornelia and John were going to Vermont and they did not ask Constantine to watch me. Instead, (are you ready for this?) they decided to put me in a kennel! I almost had a stroke when they told me they were actually going to go through with that. Evidently, Constantine was not available at the moment, and someone had told Cornelia that this particular kennel was a clean and safe place for me. I was like, "I don't care how safe this place is supposed to be, I'm not going and that's final!" But Cornelia and John had checked the place out beforehand and decided to try it. Or so they say! In actuality, it was I that had to try it, and all they had to do was pay for it! And so, as it always was, against my best wishes, Cornelia and John brought me to this "safe" kennel, where I was going to be for a few days, with other dogs. Cornelia made me laugh when she told me to "be a good dog" and try to get along with every-one else there. "Be a good dog!" Indeed!

First of all, that kennel had just way too many other dogs there. I didn't like competing with all of them for quality time spent on my behalf. The kennel had some guy named Dave, who was supposed to be taking care of me; feeding me, walking me, that sort of thing. When I first saw him, I barked to him, "Look, buster. Nobody touches me except my masters." But he didn't listen, and when I saw he wasn't afraid of me, I figured I better try to get along with him, just in case I needed him to protect me from all those other mutts that were there.

There were some mean characters in that kennel with me. Some of them barked at me, called me some mean names. Some of them dared to get fresh with me and threatened to eat my dog food when I wasn't looking. But that was all right, because I got back at them. At night, when everyone was trying to sleep, I barked my head off keeping everybody awake. That was my way of saying, "You guys would not leave me alone in peace, so you're not going to have any peace! So there!" In fact, I barked so much, that by the time Cornelia and John came back from their vacation to get me, my throat was so sore from doing all that barking, I almost had laryngitis! But it was well worth it, because all the other dogs stopped picking on me. Dave and the other people at the kennel started taking better care of me; by giving me a bath and a haircut. (Actually, they had to give everyone there a bath, because some of the other dogs were very messy, and didn't care much for their own personal hygiene.)

When Cornelia and John finally did come back to pick me up, Cornelia had asked how I was, and the kennel people told her I was LOUD! Well, what do you expect? I wasn't about to turn the other cheek, at least not to these other mongrels. They got what they deserved, an earful from me. Hey, if they couldn't take the heat, tell them to take a nice, cold bath! Anyway, I was glad Cornelia and John came when they did. My throat was hurting me, and within a few days of being back home again, my throat felt better, and I was able to rest anytime I wanted, in the environment that I felt safe in, and that was home, and not anywhere else.

I have had this annoying pain in my left shoulder lately, and it has caused me some discomfort in my left leg. Every once in a while, I would walk with a limp, or I would be forced to lift up my left front paw. Cornelia and John have noticed this, and so had Constantine when he would come over for a visit. Everyone would be saying, "Oh, you poor dog. You're getting old," and all this kind of stuff. I'm like, "Please, spare me your pities," but even so, Cornelia made an appointment for me to see the veterinarian. (I call him "the animal quack!") Anyway, we went to see him a few weeks later, and he checked me out. He said I had the beginning stages of arthritis in my neck. I was thinking, "I have what? Arthur who?" I couldn't believe it. How could I have arthritis? That's for older people and older dogs. I'm still a young puppy at heart, even though I am almost twelve years old, in human years. Man, where did the time go? It seemed like it was just yesterday that I wanted to bite John in the you-know-where for scaring me that one time in Constantine's first apartment on Staten Island. And to reflect on that now, that was almost six years ago!

Anyway, I now have to take these pills for my arthritis called Glucosamine. They are supposed to contain Vitamin C. You should see the size of these pills. They're so big, a horse couldn't even swallow one!

When Cornelia first started to give them to me, I would look at it first, sniff it, sit down and then give Cornelia a look that would translate to, "Well, what do you want me to do with that?"

Cornelia would tell me, "Come on, Bruce. Eat it."

Eat that? Are you out of your mind? I couldn't eat that if you paid me. No one, not even Janet Jackson, could make me eat that. Then Cornelia got smart. The veterinarian told her I could have a little cream cheese with those pills. So, Cornelia would cut the pill in half, cover one of the halves with the cream cheese and toss it to me. She knows I'll catch it, especially if it has a lot of the cheese on it. Then, once I am done with that half, Cornelia would do the same thing with the other half. In this way, I am taking my medicine and at the same time, getting a treat. Otherwise, you can forget about me eating those horse pills. Of course, I planned it that way. My being stubborn paid off. I'm telling you, you have to get up pretty early in the morning to put one over on me.

Every day I learn a new word in the English language, and today's new word is reincarnation. By definition, it means "a continuation of soul after death in a new body". I hear this word used a lot on television, whether it is a religious show or on *The Golden Girls.* I have heard people who really don't believe in it say that if it were possible, they would like to come back to life as another person, or as an animal, such as a dog, or a cat or a fish. I can see why people would want to be like us dogs, because we are so lovable and loyal, or as a fish, so as to explore the seas, but to come back as a cat? You must be kidding! Who in their right minds would want to be like those sneaky snakes? I would rather stay deceased than come back as a cat. Personally, I would come back as another dog rather than come back as anything else, and that includes coming back as a human being. We dogs may live boring lives, but it sure beats going to school for at least twelve years, then go to work for another forty years. And get married, buy a house, and have children, and so on. Too much stress; too much pressure. And the bottom line is always about money. Who really needs all those headaches? Not me! Just give me a nice home to live in, feed me on a regular basis and I will provide you with some good old-fashioned, tender loving canine care. Besides, with the way you humans are messing up this world with your fighting wars, and your pollutions, and abusing the planet's natural resources, I wouldn't be able to sleep at night knowing that I had involuntarily destroyed a forest by building a house.

Cornelia and John had been concerned about my overall health for a while now, particularly because I am almost twelve years old and have arthritis. More than anything, they have been concerned about my breath. They have been making some pretty snide remarks when I "kiss" or lick them. Both Cornelia and John have been saying how bad my breath smells. I'm like, "Well, what do you want me to do? With my paws, I can't brush my teeth in the morning the way you humans can. And I am certainly not going to let you humans touch my teeth, either."

So guess what happened! On my latest visit with the veterinarian, Cornelia ratted on me and told that dog quack that I have bad breath! The vet then put me on the table, and with Cornelia holding me, he pulled my mouth open, looked at my teeth and said I have a lot of tartar on my teeth. He also said I could have an infected tooth. So, he and Cornelia made arrangements for me to come back to have my teeth cleaned and to remove that bad tooth. I was thinking, *Over my dead body will you do that!* I pleaded with Cornelia and John not to go ahead with this. But against my best wishes, they made the arrangements to go along with it. Oh, those two traitors! The things I have done for them, and this is how they reward me!

I went back to the veterinarian just a few days after the appointment was made. There I was, sitting in the waiting room with Cornelia and John, waiting for that quack to come and take me. One by one, the vet's other patients marched into the office; all dogs, some as small as me, some bigger than Ralph Kramden of *The Honey-mooners*. Then, one lady came to the office with her pet cat. All of us animals were just sitting there looking at each other, wondering who was going to be next. Then, the vet came out and said, "Bruce!" I must have jumped up a good two feet! And just like that, Cornelia handed me to the quack. The two of them spoke for a few minutes, and the vet told Cornelia and John to come back in a few hours. I was like, "What?!?" I know I have hair in my ears, but did I hear right? Come back in a few hours? You mean, Cornelia and John are really going to leave me in the hands of these Doctor Frankensteins, and what, come back after my brain had been put back into my head the wrong way? And with that, Cornelia tells me to be a good boy for the vet. I looked at her saying to myself, has she had a few headaches lately? Then she and John leave the office, and there I was, too helpless to free myself, and being carried to another room to be tortured.

Actually, the procedure went better than I thought it would. The vet put me under general anesthesia, and while I was in dreamland being cuddled by Halle Berry, the doctor went to work on me. The details are fuzzy; I do not remember what really happened. But they did remove one bad tooth and cleaned the rest. When I finally came to about two hours later, my mouth felt sore, my tummy felt sick and my head was spinning faster than a speeding bullet. I just closed my eyes again and concentrated on Halle. Here was a woman who starred in a James Bond movie after winning an Academy Award in another. I didn't really care how many movies she made or will make, as long as she was with me in my hour of need.

Then the vet came to me and told me I had to get up and start walking again before Cornelia and John came back. I'll tell you, my legs felt like rubber. But as soon as I started walking, they felt better. I looked at myself in a mirror, and looked as though I was in a fight. My hair was all over the place! Just then, the vet came and brought me out to Cornelia and John. Boy, was I happy to finally see those two! Come on, guys. Pay that quack's bill and let's get out of here. This place makes me want to puke; which incidentally, was what I actually did in the car on the ride home.

I'll say this much about the veterinarian. Even though I don't like going to him, because I am afraid of him, he does take good care of me. Within days, I was feeling better, and my mouth didn't hurt as much. My breath also felt better. That's good; now Cornelia and John don't have to hold their noses when I lick them, or give them kisses.

One thing I will admit to, though, and that is I find myself getting more and more paranoid about going for a ride in the car. I know Cornelia and John are safe drivers, but I just can't help myself. It seems once I'm in a car and the car is moving, I gotta get out. My heart starts racing, my breathing gets heavier; and this is before they even turn on the ignition. Once that is turned on, then the fun really begins. And because I act this way, I have to sit in the back seat with Cornelia holding on to me; otherwise, I would be responsible for a major car crash.

I guess the combination of being in a small closed environment, and one that moves, mind you, is just not my cup of tea. In order to calm me down just a wee bit, a few windows have to be opened so I can get some air. I like to think of this as being in a submarine a few hundred feet below sea-level. But once Cornelia and John reach their destination, I can get out, walk on dry land, kiss the earth and go to the bathroom on John's shoes. (I made that last part up.) Seriously, I get so dehydrated, that I really do have to go to the bathroom, and then drink a lot of water. Then, and only then, would I be able to calm down. That is, until we get ready to go back home. Then the routine starts all over again. I'm like, "Guys! You know I don't like to go anywhere, so why bother taking me? Why don't you have so-and-so come to our house (notice, I said OUR) so they can see me? Wouldn't that be easier?" Honestly, you humans just don't think!

But I also notice that Cornelia and John would have to go to someplace and leave me home on purpose. That's o.k., I really don't mind. I would prefer to stay at home anyway. Then Cornelia would say to me, "Would you like to come with us and see so-and-so?" Then, I would look at her and say, "No thanks. I would rather stay home and catch some flies."

During the week, while John is at work, Cornelia is working, too; taking good care of the house. She would vacuum the rugs, do laundry, dust the furniture, do a little food shopping, prepare dinner for the three of us at night, and wash the dishes. On weekends, when John is home, he and Cornelia would do a few errands together that would include doing a major grocery shopping. Then they would come home and have lunch together. Then, John would go out and cut the grass, do some weeding, and some other odds and ends around the house that Cornelia could not do by herself. (Some of which would require heavy lifting.) And all I would do, is lay there and watch.

Honestly, watching Cornelia and John do all that work in their house wears me out. I get exhausted just thinking what chores they would do. When John cuts the grass with that lawnmower, I would just sit there and watch what areas he would miss; then I would think of a way to tell him politely that he missed that spot. By the time I would finally be able to tell him, he would have already seen where he missed and had that spot taken care of. And the same goes for Cornelia when she vacuums the rug. She would miss a spot, and before I could say, "woof," she would see where she missed and go over it again. In a way, I am supervising Cornelia and John on their house chores and would make sure they don't miss anything. Otherwise, I would be forced to say something. I tell ya, it's not easy!

I would like to take the time now to give you an update on the rest of the family. Ted and Ourania are still living comfortably in Toms River, as is Constantine. As of now, Constantine is doing odd jobs painting other people's houses. He is also dating a nice woman named

Michelle. Gregory and Dorothy and Christina just recently moved from Greece back to the States. They are currently looking for a new house in North Carolina, where Greg will be working as a manager of a Blockbuster Video store. They also have a new dog, named Sandy. Nick and Dena and Rocky are still living in Old Bridge. Nick and Dena are working in New York, so they commute back and forth every day by bus. John's mother just recently passed away, and his dad still lives by himself on Staten Island. Everyone on John's side of the family takes turns checking up on him. John's brother, Jim, lives in Pennsylvania with his family and their dog, Zoey, who is about eleven months old. As for myself, I'm doing well. Just as long as I keep Cornelia and John on their toes and out of harm's way, everything will be all right. I've seen a lot in the almost twelve years that I have been around, and I am sure to see a lot more in the next few years to come. And if you should ever need some advice; well, here it is: Relax, and take it easy. As a wise old hound once said, "You're only here for just a short visit, so you might as well stop and smell the flowers along the way, so you can appreciate all that nature has given us. Never mess with good old Mother Nature, because if you do, Mother Nature has a way of getting back at you."